# POWERSHELL FOR BEGINNERS

*THE COMPLETE GUIDE TO MASTER WINDOWS POWERSHELL SCRIPTING*

*By:*

CHASE CLARKE

# CONTENTS

WHAT IS POWERSHELL? ------------------------------------------------------- 4

HISTORY OF POWERSHELL ---------------------------------------------------- 5

HOW TO START POWERSHELL ------------------------------------------------ 7

LEARNING POWERSHELL FROM THE START ---------------------------------12

POWERSHELL SCRIPT ------------------------------------------------------------14

WHAT IS POWERSHELL ISE? --------------------------------------------------16

POWERSHELL CONCEPTS--------------------------------------------------------17

DIFFERENCE BETWEEN POWERSHELL AND CMD? ---------------------------20

THE POWERSHELL PIPELINE----------------------------------------------------55

POWERSHELL WILDCARDS --------------------------------------------------------57

POWERSHELL PROVIDERS AND MODULES ----------------------------------60

SYNCHRONOUS Vs ASYNCHRONOUS----------------------------------------70

WHAT MAKES A POWERSHELL OBJECT? ---------------------------------72

OTHER POWERSHELL COMMANDS --------------------------------------------78

UNDERSTANDING OF POWERSHELL FOREACH LOOP AND FOREACH-OBJECT -------------------------------------------------------------------------83

WINDOWS POWERSHELL PROVIDERS --------------------------------------90

# WHAT IS POWERSHELL?

Windows PowerShell is an item situated robotization motor and scripting language. It is primarily aimed at system administrators. It causes I.T. experts, to control and mechanize the administration of the Windows operating system and other applications.

Some compelling new concepts have been introduced to help you expand the knowledge acquired and the scripts created in the Windows command prompt and Windows Script Host environments.

It combines the flexibility of scripts, the speed of the command line, and the performance of a GUI-based administration tool. You can solve problems efficiently by helping the system administrator eliminate future manual hours. We will review all the important aspects you should know to enable you to learn PowerShell.

**Why use Powershell?**

Here are some of the main reasons to use Powershell:

- Powershell offers an all-around coordinated order line understanding for the operating system.
- PowerShell permits full access to different types in the .NET Framework.
- Powershell is classified as trusted by system administrators.
- PowerShell is an easy way to modify server and workstation components
- It addresses system administrators by creating a simpler syntax

# HISTORY OF POWERSHELL

The first version 1.0 of PowerShell was released in 2006. Today, PowerShell is in version 5.1. PowerShell's features and hosting environments have grown significantly over the course of the year and version.

See the version history of Powershell:

PowerShell version 1 supported local administration of Windows Server 2003

PowerShell 2.0 has been integrated into Windows 7 and Windows Server 2008 R2. This version supports remoting and extends PowerShell functions such as transactions, background processes, events and debugging, etc.

PowerShell 3.0 was discharged as an inside piece of the Windows the board system. It has been introduced on Windows 8 and Windows Server 2012. You can include and plan employments, meeting network, programmed stacking of structures and so forth.

PowerShell 4.0 was sent with Windows 8.1 and Windows Server 2012 R2. Support for desired state configuration, advanced debugging and network diagnostics has been added in this release.

PowerShell 5.0 has been released as part of the Windows Management Framework 5. The features offered in this version are remote debugging, class definitions and .NET enumerations, etc.

**Powershell Functionality**

PowerShell Remoting: PowerShell can be used to call scripts and cmdlets on a remote computer.

Background jobs: scripts or pipelines can be called asynchronously. Jobs can be performed on the local computer or multiple remote-controlled computers.

Transactions: Activate the cmdlet and allow developers to run it.

Evening: with this command, you can listen, forward and react to administrative and system events.

Network File Transfer: Powershell provides native support for priority, asynchronous and limited file transfer between computers using Background Intelligent Transfer Service (BITS) technology.

# HOW TO START POWERSHELL

PowerShell is pre-installed on all the latest versions of Windows. We need to start PowerShell so we can do the following:

Step 1) Search for PowerShell on Windows, choose and click

Step 2) Open the Power Shell window

**PowerShell cmdlet**

A cmdlet, also known as a let command, is a compact command used in the Windows-based PowerShell environment. PowerShell calls these cmdlets at the command prompt. You can create and invoke the cmdlets command using the PowerShell APIS.

**Cmdlet vs. command**

Cmdlets differ from commands in other command shell environments in the following ways:

- Cmdlets are objects of the .NET Framework class. They cannot be performed separately
- Cmdlets can be created from a dozen lines of code
- The cmdlets do not handle analysis, formatting of the output and presentation of errors
- The cmdlet process works for objects. Therefore, text data flow and objects cannot be passed as pipeline output
- Cmdlets are record-based, so only one object is processed at a time

Most of the PowerShell features come from cmdlets, which are always in verb-noun format and not in the plural. Also, the return objects of the cmdlet are not text. A cmdlet is a series of commands that span more than one line and are put away in a book record with the augmentation .ps1.

A cmdlet is always composed of a verb and a noun, separated by a dash. Some of the verbs you use to learn PowerShell are:

- Get — To get something
- New — To create something
- Stop — To stop things that are running
- Start — To run something

The following is a rundown of significant PowerShell Commands:

Out — To output something

Set — To define something


**Model**: Display help data about the direction Format-Table

Get-Command – Get data about anything that can be conjured

Get-Help Format-Table

**Model**: To create a summary of cmdlets, limits presented in your machine

Get-Command

Get-Service: Finds all cmdlets with the word 'administration' in it

**Model**: Get all administrations that start with "vm"

Get-Service "vm*"

Get-Member: Show what should be possible with an object

**Model**: Get individuals from the vm forms

Get-Service "vm*" | Get-Member

**Different Commands:**

Get-Module - Shows bundles of commands

Get Content - This cmdlet can take a record and process its substance and accomplish something with it

Get-get - Finds all cmdlets beginning with the word 'get-

**Model**: Create a Folder

New-Item - Path 'X:\Chase99' - ItemType Directory

Yield

**Powershell Data types:**

Boolean - True or false condition

Byte - An 8-bit unsigned whole number from to 255

Char - A 16-bit unsigned number from 0 to 63,535. For Example, 1,026

Date - A calendar date such as August 2, 2018

Decimal - A 128-bit decimal value, such as 5.18129265

Double-A - A double-precision 64-bit floating-point number. This is another type of decimal value but has a very narrower range of values compared with a decimal data type.

Integer - A 32-bit signed while number from 2,147,483.648 to 2,146,483.647. Such as 15 or -1932.

Long - A 64-bit signed the whole number. This is like an integer but holds far bigger value. 9,238,372,039,854,775.877.

Object - Description

Short - a 16-bit unsigned number. This data type is similar to integer but holds far fewer values. It can only sort values from -32,768 to 32,767

Single-A - A single-precision 32-bit floating-point number. This is a very similar data type, just like double. However, it holds fewer values, such as 20.3654

String - A grouping of characters, which is also just called text.


**Extraordinary Variables:**

Extraordinary Variable Description

$Error: A variety of mistake objects which show the latest blunders

$Host: Display the name of the current facilitating application

$Profile: Stores whole way of a client profile for the default shell

$PID: Stores the procedure identifier

$NULL: Contains unfilled or NULL worth.

$False: Contains FALSE worth

$True: Contains TRUE worth

# LEARNING POWERSHELL FROM THE START

O pen a PowerShell console by pressing Windows + R, typing PowerShell.exe, and pressing 'Enter.'

- Enter the following command: Update-Help-force (You can run a command by pressing 'Enter.' You may need to restart PowerShell as an administrator if this command does not work without error messages.)

- Run the command: Get-Help on *

- Choose an item that you find interesting.

- Repeat the Get-Help command with the name of the element you want to read. (You can use the Tab key to complete partially entered commands and parameters to save the entry.)

- If you want to see which commands are currently available, use the 'Get-Command' command.

- The Get-Help command works for all of these commands (including Get-Help) and the information sections. It contains information on what the command does and what parameters the command can supply and what they do.

- Experiment, try things, learn, use Google whenever you want/need. Then repeat.

- Don't forget: If you're not sure what a command does, add the – 'WhatIf' parameter before running it. Any command that does not support it will display an error message, while commands that support it will print messages indicating what the command would have done without actually doing anything.

- The 'Confirm' parameter is similar to -WhatIf but poses a question for each secondary operation to be performed, which will be performed only if you answer 'Yes.'

- Oh, if you have experience with MS-DOS or Unix, try some of their commands (like dir or ls). They are not the same in PowerShell, but there are many alias definitions with which users of other command-line processors can work at home. (Try Get-Alias to see all this.)

- When finished, type 'exit' and press Enter. Or use Alt-F4. Or close the PowerShell console like any other window.

# POWERSHELL SCRIPT

Powershell scripts are saved in the .ps1 file. By default, you cannot run a script simply by double-clicking on a file. This protects the system from accidental damage. To run a script:

Right-click on it and click 'Run with PowerShell.'

There is also a policy that restricts script execution. You can view this policy by running the Get-Execution Policy command.

You will receive one of the following problems:

Limited: Scripts are not allowed. This is the default, so it appears for the first time when you run the command for the first time.

AllSigned: Scripts signed by a trusted developer can be executed. With this setting, a script requires confirmation that you actually want to run before it'll run.

RemoteSigned: You can run unsigned scripts or scripts signed by a trusted developer.

Unlimited: You can run any script you want to run.

**Steps to change the execution policy:**

**Step 1**: Open an elevated PowerShell command prompt. Right-click on PowerShell and click 'Run as administrator.'

**Step 2**: Enter the Following directions:

Get-ExecutionPolicy

Set-execution strategy unlimited

Enter 'Y' in the brief

Get-ExecutionPolicy

First PowerShell Script

In a notepad compose the accompanying order

Compose Host, "Hi, Chase99!"

PowerShell Scripts have an augmentation ps1. Save the document as FirstScript.ps1

In Powershell, call the content using the order 'X:\FirstScript.ps1'

# WHAT IS POWERSHELL ISE?

The Windows PowerShell (ISE) integrated scripting environment is the standard editor for Windows PowerShell. In this ISE, you can run commands, write tests and debug scripts in a Windows GUI environment. You can perform multiline editing, syntax coloring, tab completion, selective execution and many other things.

Windows PowerShell ISE additionally permits you to run directions in a support region. However, panes that allow you to view the source code of the script and other tools that can be integrated with ISE are also supported.

You can even open multiple script windows simultaneously. This is especially useful when debugging a script that uses functions defined in other scripts or modules.

The same script that we created in the editor can be created in ISE.

- Glue code into notepad
- Spare Script
- Use F5 to run the Content
- Watch yield in the reassure

Sample:

The accompanying code will give a Free Virtual Memory in your machine

Get-WmiObject - Class Win32_OperatingSystem – ComputerName localhost |

Select-Object - Property CSName,FreeVirtualMemory

# POWERSHELL CONCEPTS

Cmdlets are compilations commands written in .NET languages such as VB or C #. Designers can expand the arrangement of cmdlets by stacking and composing PowerShell snap-ins.

### Functions

Functions are directions written in the PowerShell language. It can be developed without using another IDE, such as Visual Studio and developers.

### Scripts

Scripts are text files on the hard drive with the extension .ps1

### Applications

Applications are existing Windows programs.

What if the cmdlet is asked not to run it but to tell you what would happen if the cmdlet were to run?

'Confirmation' instructs the cmdlet to request before running the command.

'Verbose' provides a higher level of detail.

'Investigate' instructs the cmdlet to give troubleshooting data.

'ErrorAction' instructs the cmdlet to play out specific activities when an error occurs. The permitted actions are continued, interrupted, tacitly continued and interrogated.

'Error variable' specifies the variable that contains information about the error.

'OutVariable' instructs the cmdlet to use a specific variable to store the output information.

OutBuffer instructs the cmdlet to save the specified number of objects before the next cmdlet is called in the pipeline.

The advantages of using PowerShell scripts are:

- PowerShell scripts are very powerful and can do a lot in fewer lines.
- Variables are declared in the form $ <variable>
- Variables can be used to store the output of commands, objects and values.
- It is not necessary to specify the 'type' of a variable.

**Command Prompt**

PowerShell is profoundly coordinated into the Windows working framework. It offers an intuitive order line interface and a scripting language.

The order brief is the standard direction line interface given by Microsoft. It is a straightforward Win32 application that can cooperate and speak with all Win32 questions in the Windows working framework.

PowerShell uses so-called cmdlets. It can be called in the runtime environment or automation scripts.

Neither of these features offers anything other than the command prompt.

PowerShell displays them as objects. This allows you to forward the output to other cmdlets.

The command prompt or even the * nix shell, the output generated by a cmdlet, is not just a flow of text, but a collection of objects.

PowerShell is very advanced in terms of functions, skills and internal functions and the command prompt is very simple.

**Powershell applications**

Today, PowerShell is the ideal choice for IT administrators because it simplifies administration and effort in large corporate networks. Let's say you are running a large network with over four hundred servers. Presently you need to actualize another security arrangement. This security arrangement relies upon specific help that must be running on these servers.

You can securely log in to any server and see if this service is installed and running or not. In this case employees have to spend a lot of time on this unproductive process.

However, if you are using PowerShell, you can perform this task in minutes. This is because the whole process is done with a single script that collects information about the services running on the servers.

# DIFFERENCE BETWEEN POWERSHELL AND CMD?

Powershell

1. Integrates directly into the .Net framework; you have easy access to real programming libraries directly into your code.

2. Integrates directly into WMI – WMIC, others are not required

3. Treat objects rather than text strings; it is not necessary to try to analyze the textual output of various commands and hope that they don't change in a future version and damage the.BAT files.

4. Consistent command syntax: is / S or / R occurring through subdirectories? It depends on the command or the program. In PowerShell, it is always an acknowledgment.

5. Detectable commands: How often did you have to perform some Google / Bing functions to find the name of a command-line program or an integrated command? Now you can find all the commands related to a topic using the Get-Help command.

6. The alias and command completion is very intelligent - although the PowerShell commands are quite tedious, eg. 'Get-ChildItem' instead of 'DIR.' In practice, you can use 'gci' instead, and the command-line options can be reduced to the first unique substring.

7. Perfect integration with XML or JSON (see, for example, ConvertTo-JSON) - Allows you to format the data that can be used by other programs,and vice versa.

8. Huge collections of work command to copy from; someone has probably already done what you're trying to do.

9. Package creation and distribution of PowerShell code via modules, including help and security through code signing.

**Benefits of learning PowerShell programming**

The main advantages of Powershell are:

It is already (mainly) available on Windows computers. H. It is not necessary to install additional elements or create settings to make it work, as usually happens with Java, Python, C #, Ruby, etc. It's like a simulated version of the venerable Windows command prompt that you can use immediately. However, if you primarily work on non-Windows computers, you may also stop reading here since Powershell is irrelevant outside of the Windows ecosystem (as far as I know).

It is powerful: it can carry out most of the tasks that the full languages of the computer can perform, such as: Creating text files, backups, analyzing files, etc. And it's built into Windows, which means it can be used as an active directory etc.

It is easy to use. It is a scripting language and unlike Bash, Perl, or even Java (where you need to insert multiple lines of code to do the same thing).

If you are a system administrator/work in IT support and primarily support Windows-based systems, you will probably want to invest time and energy in learning Powershell, as this can help automate many of the routine tasks and problems you face,

**Other benefits**

Consistency:

A scripting solution always executes the same script

No risk of typos, forgetting how to do the job or doing the job wrong

Audit Trail:

There are many activities where an audit trail would be useful, e.g. B. what activity was performed? Important results, errors that occurred during the execution of the activity and who performed it? etc.

Time change:

With scripts, you can do a job much faster than the GUI

PowerShell is easy to adapt, learn, and use as no programming skills are required.

PowerShell is here to stay:

It is not possible to deliver all server products without the PowerShell interface.

In many cases, Microsoft uses it to create GUI management consoles for its products. Some tasks cannot be performed in the GUI and can only be performed in PowerShell.

Microsoft has clarified that PowerShell will remain and PowerShell form 2 isn't just used for Windows Server 2008 R2 and Windows 7 yet is actuated as a matter of course.

This gives us incredible flexibility. Filter, sort, measure, group, view or perform other actions on objects as they pass through the pipeline. Work with properties and methods instead of raw text.

PowerShell is very important for Windows system administration because most Microsoft products can be integrated with it. It is easy to read and understand and no programming background is required to control it.

PowerShell is an object-based and non-text-based scripting language.

PowerShell is an open source and it can be used to create GUI.

This can also be useful for normal users as you can:

Automate tasks like cleaning and storage

Conduct advanced searches on your computer

Automate daily / monthly reports

Copy files from one location to another

Automate GUIs

**Start with the PowerShell commands**

PowerShell commands are called cmdlets. These cmdlets are the driving force behind their practical functions. From directions that improve the general Windows experience to directions helpful for development, developers should know dozens of important commands. We have compiled this list as a practical reference for those who are just starting to use the power of PowerShell, as well as for those who wish to improve their PowerShell experience.

In addition to the cmdlets, there are dozens of parameters and methods that you can use to get the most out of your scripts. The WhatIf parameter is especially valuable for testing PowerShell contents without really running them. There are usually several parameters and methods available for each command. The following commands are a good starting point for any developer. However, to take full advantage of the benefits, you also need to master parameters and other methods.

**Basic PowerShell cmdlet**

These basic PowerShell commands are useful for obtaining information in various formats, configuring security and creating basic reports.

## 1. Get command

Get-Command is an easy-to-use reference cmdlet that calls all the commands available for use in the current session.

Just enter this command:

get-command

The output looks like this (@MS_ITPro):

CommandType

Name

Definition

-----------

----

----------

Cmdlet

Add-Content

Add-Content [-Path] <String[...

Cmdlet

Add-History Add-History [[-InputObject] ...

Cmdlet

Add-Member

Add-Member [-MemberType]

## 2. Get-Help

The Get-Help command is essential for all PowerShell users and gives you snappy access to the data you have to run and works with every single accessible command.

For example, type the following (@jp_jofre):

Get-Help [[-Name] <String>] [-Path <String>] [-Category <String[]>] [-Component <String[]>]

[-Functionality <String[]>] [-Role <String[]>] [-Examples] [<CommonParameters>]

## 3. Set-ExecutionPolicy

By default, Microsoft disables scripts to prevent malicious scripts from running in the PowerShell environment. However, developers want to be able to write and execute scripts so they can use the Set-Execution Policy commands to control the security level for PowerShell contents. To set one of four security levels:

Limited: This is the default security level that blocks the execution of PowerShell scripts. At this security level, commands can only be entered interactively.

All signed: This level of security allows scripts to run only if signed by a trusted publisher.

Remote access: In this level of security, you can run all locally created PowerShell scripts. Remotely created scripts can only be executed if a reputable publisher has signed them.

Unrestricted: As the name implies, the unrestricted level of security allows all scripts to run by removing all restrictions from the execution policy.

If you work in an unknown environment, you can easily find out which current execution policy is in use with this command:

Get-ExecutionPolicy

**4. Get-Service**

It is likewise valuable to realize which administrations are introduced on the framework. You can, without much of a stretch, access this data with the accompanying command:

Get-Service

The output looks like this (@MS_ITPro):

Status Name DisplayName

------ ---- -----------

Running AdobeActiveFile... Adobe Active File Monitor V4

Stopped Alerter Alerter

Running ALG Application Layer Gateway Service

Stopped AppMgmt Application Management

Running ASChannel Local Communication Channel

If you need to know if a particular service is installed, you can add the '-Name' option and the name of the service. Windows then displays the status of the service. Besides, filter functions can be used to return a certain subset of the currently installed services. The following example returns data from the Get-Service command that was passed to the Where-Object cmdlet, which then filters anything other than the stopped services:

Get Assistance | Where-Object {$ _. State -eq "stopped"}

## 5. ConvertTo-HTML

If you have to remove information that you can use in a report or send it to another person, ConvertTo-HTML is a simple method to do it. To use it, pass the yield of another order to the Convert to HTML direction and use the '-Property' choice to determine what yield properties you need in the HTML document. You likewise need to give the document a name.

For instance, the accompanying code makes a HTML page that runs down PowerShell assumed names in the present format:

PS C:\> get-alias | convertto-html > aliases.htm

PS C:\> invoke-item aliases.htm

Reward: The

Fare CSV

The cmdlet works similarly yet sends out information to a.CSV record instead of HTML. Use 'Select-Object' to determine which properties you need to be remembered for the output.

## 6. Get-EventLog

PowerShell allows you to analyze your computer's event logs using the Get-EventLog cmdlet. Several parameters are available. Use the '-Log' option followed by the log file name to view a specific log. For instance, you can use the accompanying order to see the application log:

Get-EventLog -Log "application"

In this post (@nextofwindows), you can find other examples of Get-EventLog in action. Other general parameters are (@ SS64):

-Verbose

-Debug

-ErrorAction

-ErrorVariable

-WarningAction

-WarningVariable

-OutBuffer

-OutVariable

## 7. Get-Process

Similar to getting a list of available services, it is often helpful to get a quick list of all the processes currently running. With the 'Get-Process' command, you always have this information at your fingertips.

Bonus: If you have the name or process ID, stop it with 'Stop-Process.' One example is; run this command to end all instances of

Notepad currently running (@MS_ITPro):

Notepad Stop-Process-Processname

You can also use wildcard characters, e.g. The following terminates all instances of Notepad and all other processes that begin with the word 'note':

End process name Note *

**8. Clear history**

What if you want to delete the entries from the command history? Simple; use the 'Clear-History' cmdlet. You can also use it to clear fewer commands, for example, the following command deletes commands that contain 'help' or end with 'command' (@MS_ITPro):

PS C: \> Clear history command * help *, * command

To add entries to a session, use:

Add-History

**9. Where object**

Where-Object is one of the most significant cmdlets to consider, as it will require a dataset to pass it into the pipeline for the channel (@jonathanmedd):

Get-Service | Where-Object {$_.Status -eq 'Running'}

Status Name DisplayName

------ ---- -----------

Running AdobeARMservice Adobe Acrobat Update Service

Running AppHostSvc Application Host Helper Service

Running Appinfo Application Information

Running AudioEndpointBu... Windows Audio Endpoint Builder

Running Audiosrv Windows Audio

Running BFE Base Filtering Engine

Running BITS Background Intelligent Transfer Ser...

Running BrokerInfrastru... Background Tasks Infrastructure Ser...

Running Browser Computer Browser

Running CDPSvc Connected Devices Platform Service

## 10. Set-AuthenticodeSignature

If you want to keep your work in production safe and prevent changes, use 'Set-AuthenticodeSignature' to add an Authenticode signature to a script or file.

**PowerShell directions to perform undertakings**

With regards to profitability, PowerShell can help you with commands.

## 11. For each object

The 'ForEach-Object' cmdlet plays out a procedure on every component in a predetermined arrangement of information objects. Although many cmdlets still work with any object in a collection, ForEach-Object is required for situations where you want to make other changes or apply specific formatting to all objects in a collection.

Here is a model (@MS_ITPro). In case you have to see an overview of strategy names and need to make those names 'cyan', you can endeavor the going with:

Get-Process | Write-Host $_.name -foregroundcolor cyan

The input object also, cannot be associated with the parameters for the command because of the command 'no.' For example, if the input of the pipeline or the input and its properties do not match any of the parameters, accept pipeline input.

Since the Write-Host cmdlet doesn't comprehend what you need to do with the information sent.

## 12. Clear-Content

If you want to clear the Content of an item, but want to keep the item yourself, use the 'Clear-Content' cmdlet:

Delete the contents C: \ Temp \ TestFile.txt

You can also use this command to delete the contents of all files with a specified file extension. For instance, the accompanying code frees the substance from all documents with the .txt augmentation:

Clear content path * filter *.TXT –force

You can also use wildcard characters and delete the contents of all types of files, from TXT files to DOC, XLS files and more.

## 13. Checkpoint computer

If you make important changes or run a risky experiment, you can use the Checkpoint-Computer cmdlet to set up a recovery point on your computer.

You can only use this cmdlet to create a recovery point once every 24 hours. If you run the command again, the previous restore point is preserved:

PS C:\> Checkpoint-Computer -Description "My 2nd checkpoint" - RestorePointType "Modify_Settings"

PS C:\> Get-ComputerRestorePoint | format-list

__GENUS : 2

__CLASS : SystemRestore

__SUPERCLASS :

__DYNASTY : SystemRestore

__RELPATH : SystemRestore.SequenceNumber=59

__PROPERTY_COUNT : 5

__DERIVATION : {}

__SERVER : CLIENT2

__NAMESPACE : root\default

__PATH                                                                          :
\\CLIENT2\root\default:SystemRestore.SequenceNumber=59

CreationTime : 20120202180537.316029-000

Description : My 2nd checkpoint

EventType : 100

RestorePointType : 12

SequenceNumber : 59

## 14. Compare-Object

It is supportive to have the choice of seeing two articles clearly. You can do this with 'Compare-Object,' which generates a ratio of the differences between two sets, e.g. B. (@ Marcam923):

PS G:\lee\tools> cd c:\temp

PS C:\temp> $set1 = "A","B","C"

PS C:\temp> $set2 = "C","D","E"

PS C:\temp> Compare-Object $set1 $set2

InputObject SideIndicator

----------- -------------

D =>

E =>

A <=

B <=

## 15. ConvertFrom-StringData

Use 'ConvertFrom-StringData' to convert a string with one or more pairs of values into a hash table. Here is a case of what the command resembles:

$ settings = $ TextData | ConvertFrom string

This order is valuable in different circumstances. For example, if you want to save the settings for a PowerShell script so that other users can change the settings without working directly in the script's code.

## 16. ConvertTo-SecureString

Convert a standard encrypted string to a protected string or plain text to a protected string using 'ConvertTo-SecureString.' This cmdlet is related to ConvertFrom-SecureString and Read-Host (@AdmArsenal):

ConvertTo-SecureString [-String] SomeString

ConvertTo-SecureString [-String] SomeString [-SecureKey SecureString] ConvertTo-SecureString [-String]

## 17. ConvertTo-XML

Use the 'ConvertTo-XML' cmdlet to make an XML-based portrayal of an item. This is otherwise called serialization and is a valuable procedure for filing information for later reuse: Note that your expression needs to write objects in the pipeline. Anything that uses 'Write-Host' does not write in the pipeline and, therefore, cannot be serialized. Here is an example of ConvertTo-XML in action (@PetriFeed):

Get-Service wuauserv -ComputerName chi-dc04,chi-p50,chi-core01 |

Export-Clixml -Path c:\work\wu.xml

The Export-Clixml cmdlet used in the example above is suitable for most purposes. Changes over the yield of a PowerShell articulation to XML and saves it to a document.

## 18. New-AppLocker policy

'New-AppLockerPolicy' creates a new AppLocker strategy from a rundown of record data and different standards of creative choices. There are five cmdlets in total that can be used to interact with AppLocker, including (@RootUsers_):

Get-AppLockerFileInformation: Get the information required to create the AppLocker rules from a list of files or the event log.

Get-AppLocker policy: Used to obtain a local, effective or domain AppLocker policy.

New-AppLockerPolicy: As mentioned above, this cmdlet is used to create new AppLocker policies.

Set AppLocker Policy: Sets the AppLocker policy for a specified Group Policy object.

AppLocker Policy Test: Used to determine whether a user or group of users can perform certain actions based on the policy.

## 19. New ownership of the object

'New-ItemProperty' creates a new property for an article and sets its value. For example, you can use it to create and edit registry values and data (ownership of a registry key).

In this mnaoumov.NET tutorial, you will find some useful solutions with this cmdlet (@mnaoumov).

## 20. New object

Use the 'New-Object' cmdlet to instantiate a Microsoft .NET Framework or Component Object Model (COM) object.

This example creates a new object with New-Object, stores it in a variable and then passes it to add members, adding properties or methods specified in the created object (@gngrninja):

$ourObject = New-Object -TypeName psobject

$ourObject | Add-Member -MemberType NoteProperty - Name ComputerName - Value $computerInfo.Name

$ourObject | Add-Member - MemberType

$ourObject | Add-Member - MemberType NoteProperty - Name 'working framework Version' - Value $("$($osInfo.Version) Build $($osInfo.BuildNumber)")

$ourObject | Add-Member - MemberType NoteProperty - Name Domain - Value $computerInfo.Domain

$ourObject | Add-Member - MemberType NoteProperty - Name Workgroup - Value $computerInfo.Workgroup

$ourObject | Add-Member - MemberType NoteProperty - Name DomainJoined - Value $computerInfo.Workgroup

$ourObject | Add-Member - MemberType NoteProperty - Name Disks - Value $diskInfo

$ourObject | Add-Member - MemberType NoteProperty - Name AdminPasswordStatus - Value $adminPasswordStatus

$ourObject | Add-Member - MemberType NoteProperty - Name ThermalState - Value $thermalState

## 21. New-WebServiceProxy

'New-WebServiceProxy' makes a web administration intermediary object that empowers you to utilize and deal with the web administration from inside PowerShell. This cmdlet is a delightful thing for engineers – it makes it pointless to compose a great deal of complex code to attempt to achieve something in PowerShell when you can just consider the easier functions that make it conceivable.

Here's an example:

$url = http://<webapp>.azurewebsites.net/CreateSite.asmx

$proxy = New-WebServiceProxy $url

$spAccount = "<username>"

$spPassword = Read-Host - Prompt "Enter secret key" – AsSecureString

$projectGuid = ""

$createOneNote = $false

Presently, you can run the accompanying to see a rundown of every single accessible technique:

$proxy | gm - memberType Method

## 22. New-WSManInstance

Also, to New-WebServiceProxy, New-WSManInstance makes another example of an administration asset.

New-WSManInstance winrm/config/Listener

- SelectorSet @{Address="*";Transport="HTTPS"}

-                                                        ValueSet @{Hostname="Test01";CertificateThumbprint="01F7EB07A453175 0D920CE6A588BF5"}

Look at this instructional exercise for a total bit-by-bit example of how to get the data that you must use to execute this content effectively (@jonathanmedd).

## 23. New-WSManSessionOption

'New-WSManSessionOption' makes another administration meeting hash table that is utilized as information parameters to different WS-Management cmdlets including:

Get-WSManInstance

Set-WSManInstance

Summon WSManAction

Associate WSMan

## 24. Select-Object

The 'Select-Object' cmdlet chooses the predetermined properties of a solitary item or gathering of articles. Furthermore, it can choose one of a kind items from an exhibit or a predetermined number of articles from the earliest starting point or end of a cluster.

PS > Get-Process | Sort-Object name - Descending | Select-Object - Index 0,1,2,3,4

This instructional exercise gives more data about the different ways you can utilize Select-Object (@infosectactico).

There are different cmdlets with comparable capacities, including:

Select-String: Finds messages in strings or documents.

Select-XML: Finds messages in an XML string or record.

## 25. Set-Alias

Set-Alias is an extraordinary command for improving profitability. It permits you to set a false name for a cmdlet or other direction component in the present meeting (as an easy console route), so you can work quicker.

The accompanying model sets Notepad to np in the present meeting utilizing Set-Alias (@powershellatoms):

New-Alias np c:\windows\system32\notepad.exe

Note that you can likewise tweak your PowerShell profile with the pseudonyms you regularly use (@howtogeek).

## 26. Set-StrictMode

'Set-StrictMode' creates and applies coding rules in scripts, script blocks and expressions. This is a useful command to enforce code quality and prevent you from relaxing and writing sloppy code when it's 3am and you haven't slept in two days (@adbertram).

To use it, two parameters must be considered: - Off and - Version and - Version has three potential qualities:

Form 1.0: Keeps you from using factors that have not been introduced (e.g., Option Explicit in VBScript).

Version 2.0: Prevents the use of variables that have not been initialized and also prevents the call of nonexistent properties for objects, prevents the call of a function as a method, and prevents the creation of variables without a name.

Latest version: This option allows you to select and use the latest 'StrictMode' version available. This is a good option because regardless of which version of PowerShell you are using, the latest version will be in strict mode.

## 27. Wait for the job

'Wait-Job' clears the prompt until the background processes in the current session have completed. Wait-Job does not display job output; however, it can be used in conjunction with 'Receive-job.' Multithreading is also possible in PowerShell.

```
### Start-MultiThread.ps1 ###

$Computers = @("Computer1","Computer2","Computer3")

#Start all jobs

ForEach($Computer in $Computers){

Start-Job  -FilePath  c:ScriptGet-OperatingSystem.ps1  -ArgumentList $Computer

}

#Wait for all jobs

Get-Job | Wait-Job

#Get all job results

Get-Job | Receive-Job | Out-GridView

1

2

3
```

4

5

6

7

8

9

10

11

12

13

### Start-MultiThread.ps1 ###

$Computers = @("Computer1","Computer2","Computer3")

#Start all jobs

ForEach($Computer in $Computers){

Start-Job -FilePath c:ScriptGet-OperatingSystem.ps1 -ArgumentList $Computer

}

#Wait for all jobs

Get-Job | Wait-Job

#Get all job results

Get-Job | Receive-Job | Out-GridView

## 28. Write-Progress

Who doesn't love a status bar? Monitor your progress with Write-Progress, which displays a progress bar in a Windows PowerShell command window.

Compose Progress - Id $Id - Activity $Activity - Status (&amp; $StatusBlock) - CurrentOperation $Task - PercentComplete ($Step/$TotalSteps * 100)

Cmdlet for monitoring, testing and debugging performance

There are also a number of useful cmdlets for developers to troubleshoot, test, debug and monitor. Here are some you need to know:

## 29. Debugging process

Engineers love investigating! All things considered, we like it much more when there are no bugs to fix, yet tragically this isn't generally the situation. PowerShell permits you to investigate a procedure using the Debug-Process cmdlet.

You can likewise troubleshoot forms with the investigate procedure (@MS_ITPro). You can set breakpoints or use the 'Wait-Debugger' cmdlet:

PS C:\> $job = Start-Job -ScriptBlock { Set-PSBreakpoint C:\DebugDemos\MyJobDemo1.ps1 -Line 8; C:\DebugDemos\MyJobDemo1.ps1 }

PS C:\> $job

PS C:\> Debug-Job $job

## 30. Disable-PSBreakpoint

After setting breakpoints, you now want to remove them. Use 'Disable-PSBreakpoint,' which disables breakpoints in the current console. Here is the syntax (@ActiveXperts):

Disable-PSBreakpoint [-Id] [-PassThru] [-Confirm] [-WhatIf] []

Disable-PSBreakpoint [-Breakpoint] [-PassThru] [-Confirm] [-WhatIf] []

## 31. Get counter

'Get-Counter' retrieves real-time performance counter data from Windows performance monitoring equipment. It is used to obtain performance data from local or remote computers at specified sampling intervals.

In this example, we get a set of counters with a sampling intervals for a given maximum sample (@MS_ITPro):

PS C:\> Get-Counter -Counter "\Processor(_Total)\% Processor Time" -SampleInterval 2 -MaxSamples 3

In the following example, this command retrieves some counter data from multiple computers:

The first command saves the path of the counter ** Read disk/sec ** in the $ DiskReads variable.

PS C:\> $DiskReads = "\LogicalDisk(C:)\Disk Reads/sec"

The subsequent direction utilizes a pipeline administrator (|) to send the way of the counter in the $ DiskReads variable to the ** Get-Counter ** cmdlet. The order utilizes the ** MaxSamples ** parameter to confine the yield to 10 examples.

PS C: \> $ DiskReads | Get-Counter-Computer Server01, Server02 - MaxSamples 10

## 32. Export counter

'Export-Counter' exports PerformanceCounterSampleSet objects as a counter log file. Two properties are available:

CounterSamples: Retrieve and set data for counters.

Date / Time: retrieves and sets the date and time when the sample data was recorded.

And various methods, all inherited from Object:

Equals(Object)

Finalize()

GetHashCode()

GetType()

MemberwiseClone()

ToString()

For example, the following command uses Get-Counter to collect processor time data and exports it to a .blg file using Export-Counter (@TechGenix):

Get counter "\ processor (*) \% processor time" | Export counter -Path
C: \ Temp \ PerfData.blg

## 33. Test run

You can use Test-Path to check if items exist in a specified path. For
instance, if you intend to take an alternate direction for a particular
record, you may need to check for the presence of the document to
stay away from an error.

Test path C: \ Scripts \ Archive

If the folder exists, 'True' is returned. Otherwise, 'False' is returned.

It can also be used with the paths of other PowerShell providers. For
example, if you want to know if your computer has an environment
variable called 'username,' you can use the following:

Test way Env: \ username

Test-Path works with factors, authentications, assumed names and
capacities. For more information, see this TechNet post
(@MS_ITPro).

## 34. Get-WinEvent

View Windows event logs with 'Get-WinEvent.' For a list of
available protocols, use:

Get-WinEvent -ListLog *

To check the details of a particular protocol, replace * with the name
(forward the output to the list of formats to see all the details):

Get-WinEvent -ListLog $ logname | fl *

You can also view all events in a log using the following:

Get-WinEvent -LogName System

## 35. Invoke-TroubleshootingPack

Troubleshooting packages are collections of PowerShell scripts and assemblies that you can use to troubleshoot, diagnose, and repair common system problems (@ITNinjaSite). T

Get-ChildItem C: \ Windows \ Diagnostic \ System

Then, in an elevated PowerShell window, run a troubleshooting package with the following command:

Invoke-TroubleshootingPack    (Get-TroubleshootingPack    C:    \ Windows \ Diagnose \ System \ Netzwerk)

## 36. Measurement command

If you want to plan operations in PowerShell, 'Measure-Command' is an essential cmdlet. Measures the duration of execution of a script or block of script. Here is an example (@ToddKlindt):

Measure-Command    {Mount-SPContentDatabase    –    Name wss_content_portal – WebApplication http://portal.contoso.com}

The yield is a TimeSpan object, so it contains properties like hours, minutes, seconds and so forth and it can easily adapt the output to your preferences.

## 37. Object of measurement

You may also want to know how large a particular object is. Use 'Measure-Object' to figure the numeric properties of an object, including characters, words and lines in a string object, such as B.

Text files.

Just enter the name and the type of measurement to be performed together with parameters such as (@WindowsITPro):

-Sum: adds values

-Average: calculates the average value

-Minimum: finds the minimum value

-Maximum: finds the maximum value

The following command sums the values of the VirtualMemory Dimension property for all process objects:

Get-Process | measure VirtualMemorySize -Sum

## 38. New-Event

'New-Event' is used to create a new event. A related cmdlet is 'New-EventLog,' which makes another occasion log and occasion source on a neighborhood or remote PC. If you have a mechanization motor bolstered by PowerShell, we prescribe that you set up an event log (creating a custom event log type) that logs all messages sent by PowerShell. This is an example where custom registration can be implemented in the Event Viewer.

First, create a new event log name (@BundaloVladimir):

New-EventLog -LogName Troubleshooting_Log -Source FalloutApp

Then, using the 'Write-Log' cmdlet, do the following to send messages to the new event log:

Write-EventLog -log trouble shooting_log -source FalloutApp -

EntryType-information -eventID 10 -message "FalloutApp has been installed correctly"

## 39. Work received

If you want to get the results of Windows PowerShell background processes in the current session, use 'Receive-process.' This is typically used after the startup process has been used to start a process when specific results need to be viewed.

Receive job name HighMemProcess

Read this useful tutorial on how to use Get Job and what to do if you don't seem to get any results (@proxb).

## 40. Event of the registration engine

This cmdlet is used to subscribe to events generated by the Windows PowerShell engine and the New Event cmdlet. For example, the following command signs up for an event when the current PowerShell session ends and stores information (such as the date and time) in a log file (@jonathanmedd):

Record the PowerShell. Exiting engine event

-Action {"PowerShell exits to" + (Get-Date) | External file c: \ log.txt -Append}

## 41. Register ObjectEvent

'Register-ObjectEvent' is similar to Register-EngineEvent, but does not subscribe to events generated by the PowerShell and New-Event engine, but rather to events generated by a Microsoft .NET Framework object.

Here is an example (@NetworkWorld):

Register-ObjectEvent -InputObject $ MyObject -EventName OnTransferProgress -SourceIdentifier Scp.OnTransferProgress `

-Action {$ Global: MCDPtotalBytes = $ args [3]; $ Global: MCDPtransferredBytes = $ args [2]}

Register-ObjectEvent -InputObject $ MyObject -EventName OnTransferEnd `

-SourceIdentifier Scp.OnTransferEnd -Action {$ Global: MCDPGetDone = $ True}

## 42. Remove-Event

To expel an occasion, use the 'Remove-Event' cmdlet then use 'Remove-EventLog' to clear an occasion log or unregister a source when there is a likelihood that a whole occasion log may be emptied.

Alternatively, 'Unregister-Event' unsubscribes from an event but does not delete an event from the event queue (@ SS64).

## 43. Set Debug PS

This cmdlet enables and disables script debugging features. In addition, the track level is set and StrictMode is switched.

If you use 'Set-PSDebug' at the top of the script file immediately after the param () statement (if you have one), you can avoid errors with scripts for which PowerShell does not provide enough information for troubleshooting. Here is an example (@r_keith_hill):

Set-PSDebug -Strict

PS C:\Temp> .\foo.ps1

The $ Succeded variable cannot be restored because it has not been set at this time.

A C: \ Temp \ foo.ps1: 6 character: 14

+ if ($ Succeded) <<<< {

## 44. Start-sleep

If you need to pause the movement in content or meeting, use 'Start-Suspend,' which ends the action for a specified period of time.

Start-Sleep -Seconds xxx

Start-Sleep -Milliseconds xxx

If you need to stop one or more running services, use the suspension service.

## 45. Object of the tea

When analyzing performance or code quality, it is helpful to be able to view the output of a command. If it is not the last variable in the pipeline, 'Tee-Object' sends it through the pipeline.

Here is the syntax:

Tee-Object [-FilePath] <string> [-InputObject <psobject>] [<CommonParameters>]

Variable Tee-Object <string> [-InputObject <psobject>] [<CommonParameters>]

## 46. Testing the AppLocker criteria

The Test AppLocker policy, based on the specified AppLocker policy, evaluates whether input files can be run for a particular user.

Test-AppLockerPolicy [-PolicyObject] -Path [-User] [-Filter>] []

Test-AppLockerPolicy [-XMLPolicy] -Path [-User] [-Filter] [Parameter>]

This tutorial provides further details on the available parameters and examples of Test-AppLockerPolicy in action (@powershellhelp).

## 47. ComputerSecureChannel test

This cmdlet checks and repairs the connection between a local computer and its domain. Without this command, the usual solution was to remove a computer from its domain and then reconnect it to restore the relationship. Test-ComputerSecureChannel allows you to restore the connection in less time (@WindowsITPro).

If you are logged in as a local administrator, do the following:

Test-ComputerSecureChannel  −credential  WINDOWSITPRO  \ Administrator −Repair

With Test-Connection, you can send ICMP echo (ping) request packets to one or more computers.

## 48. Trace-Command

Follow the command designs to starts to hint at a predefined direction of articulation. To utilize it, you will additionally need to use 'Get-TraceSource' so as to search for specific names using trump card characters:

PS&gt; Get-TraceSource - Name *param*

You can channel the yield to coordinate the portrayal of the example you're after. When you've recognized the conceivable follow name, you'll use 'Trace-Command' to find the solutions you need. Here's a model:

```
[CmdletBinding(DefaultParameterSetName = 'Host')]

param (

# ScriptBlock that will be traced.

[Parameter(

ValueFromPipeline = $true,

Mandatory = $true,

HelpMessage = 'Expression to be traced.'

)]

[ScriptBlock]$Expression,

Test-Path $_ -IsValid

})]

[string]$FilePath

)

begin {

if ($FilePath) {

# assume we want to overwrite trace file

$PSBoundParameters.Force = $true

} else {
```

```
$PSBoundParameters.PSHost = $true

}

if ($Quiet) {

$Out = Get-Command Out-Null

$PSBoundParameters.Remove('Quiet') | Out-Null

} else {

$Out = Get-Command Out-Default

}

}

process {

Trace-Command @PSBoundParameters | &amp; $Out

}

PS&gt; New-Alias -Name tre -Value Trace-Expression

PS&gt; Export-ModuleMember -Function * -Alias *
```

Look at this post for more subtleties on playing the analyst with Trace-Command (@PowerShellMag).

## 49. Write-Debug

'Write-Debug' composes an investigation message to reassure. At the point when you compose this incapacity or content, it doesn't do anything, of course; the messages basically lay in limbo until you either change your $DebugPreference or initiate the - troubleshoot switch when calling capacity or content. When $DebugPreference is set to 'ask' or the - troubleshoot switch is enacted, the message makes a breakpoint, giving you a simple method to fly in to investigate mode.

Take this model (@RJasonMorgan):

function Get-FilewithDebug

{

[cmdletbinding()]

Param

(

[parameter(Mandatory)]

[string]$path

)

Write-Verbose "Starting script"

Write-Debug "`$path is: $path"

$return = Get-ChildItem -Path $path -Filter *.exe -Recurse –Force

# THE POWERSHELL PIPELINE

P ipelines are seemingly the most important idea used in heading line interfaces. When used appropriately, pipelines decrease the exertion of using complex directions and make it simpler to see the progression of work for the directions. Each order in a pipeline (called a pipeline component) passes its yield to the following direction in the pipeline, thing-by-thing. Directions don't need to deal with more than each thing in turn. The outcome decreases asset utilization and the capacity to start getting the yield right away.

For instance, in the event that you use the Out-Host cmdlet to compel a page-by-page show of yield from another direction, the yield looks simply like the ordinary content shown on the screen, separated into pages:

Paging additionally decreases CPU usage since handling moves to the Out-Host cmdlet when it has a total page prepared to show. The cmdlets that go before it in the pipeline stop execution until the following page of yield is accessible.

You can perceive how channeling impacts CPU and memory utilization in the Windows Task Manager by looking at the accompanying directions:

Get-ChildItem C:\Windows - Recurse

Get-ChildItem C:\Windows - Recurse | Out-Host - Paging

**Items in the pipeline**

At the point when you run a cmdlet in PowerShell, you see content yield since it is important to speak to objects as content in a reassuring window. The content yield may not show the entirety of the properties of the article being yield.

For instance, consider the Get-Location cmdlet. On the off chance that you run Get-Location while your present area is the base of the C drive, you see the accompanying yield:

The content yield is an outline of data, not a total portrayal of the article returned by Get-Location. The heading in the yield is included by the procedure that arranges the information for the onscreen show.

At the point when you pipe the yield to the Get-Member cmdlet, you get data about the item returned by Get-Location.

# POWERSHELL WILDCARDS

The four types of Wildcard:

The * special case will coordinate at least zero characters.

The ? special case will coordinate a solitary character.

[m-n] Match a scope of characters from m to n, so [f-m]ake will coordinate phony/jake/make

[abc] Match a lot of characters a,b,c.., so [fm]ake will coordinate phony/make

Unlike the somewhat fluffy rationale of MS-DOS and the CMD shell, PowerShell trump cards are steady in their importance, so *.* will coordinate any characters followed by a period (.) followed by any characters. As such, *.* will return just records that have an expansion, not indexes.

To restore all things simply use a solitary *

While recursing a document hierarchy, it is important to use the trump card as a component of a - incorporate condition:

Get-ChildItem c:\windows - incorporate *.exe - recurse

Using a trump card character without - include:

Get-ChildItem c:\windows\*.exe - recurse

the above won't coordinate a document, for example, C:\windows\test\demo.exe

When using WMI channels, use the WMI explicit trump cards: % for at least zero characters, _ for a solitary character.

Special cases will, likewise, work inside both single and twofold statements; to forestall the trump card development use the – 'LiteralPath' parameter where accessible.

**Like for string comparison**

To play out a correlation of strings, use the – 'Like' or – 'Not Like' administrators, these examination administrators bolster the four trump cards above.

PS C:\> 'chasing the snark' - like '*snark*'

Genuine

**The – Filter parameter**

The 'Get-ChildItem' - channel parameter determines a channel in the supplier's configuration or language.

On account of a SQL supplier, the - Filter parameter may offer SQL language structure ( - Filter "WHERE Name LIKE %pattern%")

On account of the Filesystem supplier, the example is handled by Win32 API.

This implies that the channel has a similar record goal and nearly the equivalent wildcarding as CMD.exe, which uses the equivalent Win32 API. The distinction in wildcarding is that the FileSystem supplier bolsters the [] section design sentence structure, and CMD.exe doesn't.

CMD/Win32 special cases are not extremely instinctive generally for recorded reasons, and they coordinate against both short (8.3) and long filenames

For instance:

In a special case design finishing with .* the .* is overlooked.

So *.* is equivalent to * and demo*.* is equivalent to demo* this implies it will coordinate 'illustrate' a filename with no .augmentation.

The ? special case won't coordinate a dab, so while you may expect demo???? to coordinate 'demo.txt' it won't, you have to use demo.???

While coordinating augmentations, there is an inferred wildcard toward the end since short filenames are restricted to a three-character expansion, so for instance *.HTM will coordinate the document 'demo.HTML', yet *.HT won't.

In PowerShell v1, there was a noteworthy presentation advantage to using -Channel over a local PowerShell trump card, yet in v2 Microsoft added support for fractional sifting to the Filesystem supplier. This offloads as a significant part of the separating fill in as it can to the crude Win32 APIs – and afterward accomplishes all the more impressive (and right) special case coordinating on the littler arrangement of results.

This implies with regards to the Filesystem supplier, and you most likely don't need or need the - Filter parameter.

Examples

PS C:\> Get-ChildItem c:\work\*.xlsx

PS C:\> Get-ChildItem c:\work\[a-f]*.txt

PS C:\> Get-ChildItem -literalpath 'c:\work\test[1].txt'

PS C:\> Get-ChildItem -recurse -filter c:\work\demo.*

# POWERSHELL PROVIDERS AND MODULES

### Introducing Providers

Exactly when you hear the articulation 'providers,' I bet the non-fashioners among us (and I recall myself for this social occasion) start to shut out. That seems like something you do alongside making a class and starting up a for-circle with strings that go through a model view controller. Yet, that is not the situation here. Let me explain in more detail for you.

PowerShell suppliers are basically similar to drivers for the working framework, where you introduce some code to help your duplicate of Windows converse with the design's equipment, the capacity and circle subsystems and the chipset on your motherboard. The drivers contain the 'interpretation layer,' which isn't an official term, with the goal that Windows realizes how to drive the equipment and make it work for your utilization.

PowerShell suppliers are drivers for PowerShell to explore objects other than the record framework. Suppliers permit PowerShell to navigate the Registry, the File System, Windows Management Instrumentation (WMI) usefulness and that's only the tip of the iceberg. Outsiders can make suppliers: For instance, there is a SQL Server supplier that Microsoft introduces that lets you do PowerShell procedure on databases.

### How Providers Work

Suppliers take some assortment of something and make it resemble a record framework or circle drive to PowerShell. Suppliers are used by a wide range of programming bundles that help PowerShell for the organization, similar to Internet Information Services (Microsoft's webserver) and Active Directory.

This is one of PowerShell's key extensibility highlights, on the grounds that any asset or information to be overseen consistently appears like a drive. Furthermore, new directions can be included that communicate with similar information stockpiling, regardless of whether that is a database or a rundown of managerial settings for a site or a letterbox store or whatever else, truly. It's sort of cool.

How would you know what suppliers you have off the top of your head? PowerShell does, without a doubt. You can use the Get-PSProvider direction to discover them.

**Supplier Capacities and Drives**

The names of the suppliers are genuinely self-evident. PowerShell can make every one of these things appear as circle drives: Aliases, the earth (which incorporates natural factors like PATH and that's just the beginning), the FileSystem, capacities, the Registry and any characterized factors. So, I can reach in and get information or records in any of these 'places' just by cd:\ing around and adding explanations to find them at a good pace. At the point when you use a supplier, you are actually making a PSDrive, and that PSDrive is the portrayal of the capacity or asset that you are associating with as the document framework on a plate.

Capacities are a rundown of approaches to use, and things you can (and can't) do with every supplier. For the purposes of this article, we won't stress over them.

Drives, then again, are the consistent passage for suppliers. They're similar to drive mappings in Windows that you would use to make, say, Drive M: speak to an offer and its substance on another PC. So we should change 'index' to HKLM and do a registry inclining to perceive what was accessible to oversee, in which case we would use the Set-Location cmdlet to change the shell's present compartment to the holder you need.

You can see that 'dir' rattled off the primary territories of the Registry,including                 HKEY_LOCAL_MACHINE\Hardware, HKEY_LOCAL_MACHINE\Software, etc. You work the tree by using it like a document framework.

**Items**

You, use the object set of cmdlets to communicate with PSDrive suppliers. On the off chance that you keep on considering working with suppliers like working with a document framework, rather than records and envelopes, think objects. They're called things whether you're calling library objects or SQL Server databases. Object is a decent conventional term that can be used conversely.

How would you make sense of what the thing cmdlets are? Why, you'd use Get-Command, obviously!

The majority of the thing set of cmdlets have a – 'way' parameter that acknowledges special cases like *; however, this raises a significant point. Accurately, in light of the fact that suppliers support such a significant number of various kinds of capacity and assets, there might be cases in which the trump card is really a substantial, legitimate, explicit contribution for a given supplier.

In this way, for suppliers that permit the standard special case characters as lawful characters in names, you can use the - literal path rather than just - way to advise PowerShell to regard the reference bullet as a mark and not as a trump card.

How about we dive in somewhat further into 'objects.' Objects have properties, which are essential attributes of the object. In the event that I have a record, I have the date that document was made (a property), the date it was changed (a property), regardless of whether it is perused just or writeable (a property,) etc. On the off chance that I have a Registry key, I have its area (a property), its sort (a property, etc. Objects can likewise have youngster objects. Again, using the record framework model, envelopes can encapsulate organizers, and onjects inside an organizer can be documented.

**Contrasts in Suppliers Matter**

It is critical to recollect that in PowerShell, few out of every odd supplier has similar abilities. Some work when others don't, contingent upon the situation. A few suppliers let you get to unexpected things in comparison to other people; some do it in various ways, and some don't work by any stretch of the imagination.

That is the reason you generally need to consider what capacities every supplier has when building directions using a PSDrive supplier, and you should consistently recollect that when you are working with a supplier with which you are new, make certain to run Get-PSProvider to comprehend its abilities. Regardless of whether a direction appears as though it would work, the setting of the supplier wherein you are running that order matters a lot.

**A supplier model: The Registry**

The ideal approach to learn is with a hands-on model, and I can think about no superior to changing the library solely using PowerShell. Our undertaking is to kill Wi-Fi Sense in Windows 10. In spite of the fact that the Anniversary Update of Windows 10 murdered this component, generally, for any individual who hasn't moved up to the Anniversary Update, you can still track.

**Introducing modules and snap-ins**

The modules feature is where PowerShell gets its ability to address a ton of different products and services from within one shell environment. Adding modules lets PowerShell work with different features, functions and configurations from all sorts of different software, from both Microsoft and from third parties, just by importing modules full of cmdlets and their reference information, or by adding a snap-in. What are the modules? What are snap-ins? Let's do some rudimentary definition work upfront so we can get it out of the way.

Modules are nice, neat containers of PowerShell functionality that extend the namespace and targeting power of PowerShell to other pieces of hardware and software. Modules are the de-facto way of enabling PowerShell extensibility these days, and most server products that run on Windows come with modules for extending PowerShell, including all Microsoft server products from 2010 onward (and in some cases even before then).

Snap-ins - or in proper PowerShell terminology PSSnapins - is basically a set of DLL files that have accompanying XML files that contain configuration information and the text that displays when you ask for help via Get-Help. Snap-ins were part of the first release of PowerShell back in the mid-2000s, and you will see fewer of these types of extensions as time goes in as Microsoft and third parties replace them with modules. So, for that reason, in this section, I'll talk just about modules.

**Modules**

Modules are, at this point, far and away from the most common type of PowerShell extensibility feature you will see. Modules are basically containers filled with all of the information PowerShell needs to work with a given piece of hardware or software, including the commands, the libraries necessary to get those commands to work, the help text, and any configuration information that might be required. Modules exist to remedy a lot of the things that make snap-ins sort of unwieldy and difficult to consume and distribute.

**Powershell Remoting**

PowerShell Remoting lets you run PowerShell directions or access full PowerShell meetings on remote Windows frameworks. It's like SSH for getting to remote terminals on other working frameworks.

PowerShell is secured as a matter of course, so you'll need to empower PowerShell Remoting before using it. This arrangement procedure is more perplexing if you're using a workgroup rather than space—for instance, on a home system— we'll walk you through it.

**Empower PowerShell Remoting on the PC You Want to Access Remotely**

Your initial step is to empower PowerShell Remoting on the PC to which you need to make remote associations. On that PC, you'll have to open PowerShell with regulatory benefits.

In Windows 10, press Windows+X and afterward pick PowerShell (Admin) from the Power User menu.

In the PowerShell window, type the accompanying cmdlet (PowerShell's name for an order), and afterward hit Enter:

**Empower PSRemoting - Force**

This order begins the WinRM administration, sets it to begin consequently with your framework, and makes a firewall decide what permits approaching associations. The '- Force' portion of the cmdlet advises PowerShell to play out these activities without inciting you for each progression.

If your PCs are a piece of a space, you should simply make these settings. You can keep on testing your association. On the off chance that your PCs are a piece of a workgroup, most likely on a home or private company computer, more design is required.

Note: Successful remote configuration in a domain environment depends entirely on the configuration of the network. Remote servers can be automatically disabled or even enabled by a group policy organized by an administrator. Also, you may not provide the necessary requests to run PowerShell as an administrator. As always, contact your agents before trying this. You may have good reasons not to allow the practice, or you may be willing to set it up for yourself.

**Create Your Team**

If the computer is not in a domain, some steps are required to make the settings. You should already have enabled the remote control on the PC you want to connect to, as described in the previous section.

Note: To make PowerShell functions remote in a workgroup environment, you need to set up your network as a private rather than a public network

Therefore, you need to configure 'TrustedHosts' both on the PC you want to connect to and on the PC from which you want to connect so that the computers trust each other. You can do it in the intended ways.

If you are on a home network where you want to rely on a PC for remote connection, you can type the following cmdlet in PowerShell (also run as administrator).

Set-Item wsman: \ localhost \ client \ trusthosts *

The asterisk is a placeholder symbol for all PCs. If you want to limit the computer that can connect instead, you can replace the asterisk with a comma-separated list of approved IP addresses or PC computer games.

After running this command, you must restart the WinRM service for the new settings to take effect. Type the following cmdlet and press Enter:

WinRM restart service

Keep in mind that you need to run these two cmdlets on the PC you want to connect to and all the PCs you want to connect from.

**Try the connection**

After defining the PC via PowerShell Remoting, it's time to test the connection. On the PC from which you want to access the remote system, enter the following cmdlet in PowerShell (replace 'COMPUTER' with the name or IP of the remote PC) and press Enter:

Test WSMAN COMPUTER

This simple command checks whether the WinRM service is running on the remote PC. See the process is successful, the window provides information on the remote computer's WinRM service. This means that WinRM is communicated, and your PC can communicate. If the command fails, an error message is displayed instead.

**Run a single remote command**

To run a command on the remote system, use the Invoke-Command cmdlet with the following syntax:

Invoke-Command -ComputerName COMPUTER -ScriptBlock {COMMAND} -credential USERNAME

'COMPUTER' indicates the name or protected IP of the remote PC. 'COMMAND' is the command you wish to execute. 'USERNAME' is the user name with which you want to run the command as on the remote computer. You will be approached to enter a secret phrase for the username.

Here is a model I need to see the substance of the C: \ index on a remote PC with the IP address 10.0.0.22. I need to use the username 'wjgle,' so I might want to use the accompanying direction:

Summon Command - ComputerName 10.0.0.22 - ScriptBlock

{Get-ChildItem C: \} - certification wjgle

**Start A Remote Session**

If you have multiple cmdlets that you want to run on the remote PC, you can instead start a remote session instead of repeatedly entering the Invoke-Command cmdlet and remote IP address. Just type the following cmdlet and hit enter:

Enter-PSSession -ComputerName COMPUTER -Credential USER

Supplant 'PC' with the name or IP address of the remote PC and 'Client' with the name of the client account you wish to get to.

The command prompt changes to indicate the remote computer you are connected to, and you can run any number of PowerShell cmdlets directly on the remote system.

Let PowerShell do multiple things at once. You should consider PowerShell, a single-threaded application, which means that only one can be run at a time. Type a command, press Enter, and the shell waits while that command is executed. It is not possible to run a second command until the first is completed.

However, with its background work function, PowerShell can move command to a separate background thread (actually a separate background PowerShell process). This allows the command to run in the background while continuing to use the shell for other purposes.

You need to make this decision before running the command. After pressing Enter, you cannot choose to move a long-lasting command to the background. After the commands are in the background, PowerShell provides mechanisms for checking the status, getting results, etc.

# SYNCHRONOUS Vs ASYNCHRONOUS

First of all, let's tick some terms off. PowerShell executes normal commands synchronously, which means you press 'Enter' and wait for the command to complete. If you run a job in the background, it can run asynchronously. This means that you can continue to use the shell for other activities while the command is running.

There are some important differences between running commands in two ways:

At the point when you run an order synchronously, you can react to include demands. When commands are run in the background, input requests cannot be displayed. In effect, the execution of the command is stopped.

Synchronous commands generate error messages if something goes wrong. Background commands generate errors that are not displayed immediately.

If you omit a required parameter in the asynchronous command, PowerShell requests the missing information. This is not possible with a background command, so the command simply fails.

The results of the asynchronous command are displayed as soon as the results are available. With a command in the background, wait for the command to run and then get the cached results.

### Create a local job

The first type of work we deal with is perhaps the simplest; a local job. This is a command that runs pretty much completely on your neighborhood PC (with the exceptions that I will deal with in a moment), and that runs in the background.

To start one of these jobs, use the 'Start-Job' command.

Use the -script block parameter to specify the command (or commands) to be run.

PowerShell creates a default job name (Job1, Job2, etc.), or you can specify a custom job name using the -Name parameter. If the job is to be run with alternative credentials, a -credential parameter accepts a DOMAIN \ Username credential and requests the password. Instead of specifying a script block, you can specify the -FilePath parameter so that the process executes an entire script file full of commands.

# WHAT MAKES A POWERSHELL OBJECT?

If there is a key distinction among PowerShell and other scripting languages, PowerShell automatically uses objects (structured data) instead of simple strings (undifferentiated data blobs).

Consider something like a car, has:

- Colors
- Doors
- Lighting
- Wheels

These components that portray this specific item are called properties. Your vehicle can likewise get things done, and it can turn left and right, it can move to and fro; these are the strategies for the item.

Properties: Angles and subtleties of the article.

Strategies: Activities that the object can perform.

**What is the PowerShell pipeline?**

PowerShell was enlivened by numerous individuals of the extraordinary thoughts that make up 'The Unix Philosophy' - the most significant for us today are two focuses:

Let each program do one thing well. To do a new job, create new programs, not complicated old ones, adding new features.

Expect the output of each program to be another unknown program. Do not overload the output with extraneous information. Avoid strictly columnar or binary input formats. Don't insist on interactive input.

In practice, these somewhat abstract philosophical points mean that you should create many small, targeted PowerShell scripts that each perform a specific task. Whenever you set up an if / else flag, another piece of branched logic, you should ask yourself, "Would it be better than a separate script?"

For example, don't create a script that downloads a file and then analyzes the downloaded data. Create two scripts:

One which downloads the data - download.ps

A second that analyzes the data into something usable -parse.ps

To transfer data from download.ps to parse.ps, you need to route the data between the two scripts. Which is the most effective method to discover the properties and strategies for a PowerShell object.

There are too many aspects of even the simplest object in PowerShell to remember. You need a way to interactively discover what each object you encounter can do when writing your scripts.

The command needed to do this is the Get-Member cmdlet provided by Microsoft.

**How to use Get-Member**

Get-Member

[[-First name]]

[-Force]

[-InputObject]

[-MemberType]

[-Static]

[-View]

[]

Get-Member helps reassert an idea that made it difficult for me to face the transition from bash scripts to PowerShell that everything (literally everything) in PowerShell is an object. Let's take a really simple example:

1. Use the Write-Output cmdlet to write some information about our PowerShell console.

Written edition 'Hello World'

2. Assign this output to a variable called $ string

$ string = Write-Output `Hello, world

3. Pass the $ string variable (which contains 'Hello, World') to the Get-Member cmdlet

$ string | Get-Member

You will get an output similar to the following screenshot:

A list of properties and methods for this String object.

When the underlying data of the object changes, the responses of the methods and properties also change.

Some examples:

A "Hello, World" string object has a length

(property) of 13

A string object of "Hello, Earth People!" has a length of 24

Calling methods and properties with dot notation.

All methods and properties of an object must be called with a syntax called 'dot notation.' This is just an elegant way to say:

'OBJECT.PROPERTY'

Some examples:

$ String.length

13

The methods are called the same way, but brackets are

added.

$ String.ToUpper ()

Hello World!

$ String.ToLower ()

Hello World!

Neither method accepts 'arguments' – additional commands that are passed as parameters in parentheses.

$ String.Replace ('Hello,' 'Goodbye')

Goodbye, world!

With the replacement method, the first argument is what you are looking for in the 'hello' string, and the second is the one you want to replace it with.

**How to create our PowerShell objects**

Our $ string variable we created was of the System.String type - but what if we wanted to create our own object type instead of relying on the default types?

1. Create a hash table

A hash table is a key + value data store where each 'key' corresponds to a value. If you've ever received an employee number on a job or had to fill out a timesheet with the codes assigned to each company, you're familiar with the concept.

$hashtable = @{ Color = 'Red'; Transmission =

'Automatic'; Convertible = $false}

If you pass it on to Get-Members, you will now get a different list of methods and properties because it is of a different type.

(System.Collections.Hashtable instead of System.String).

2. Create a custom PowerShell object

To convert this from a hash table into a complete PowerShell object, we use a so-called 'type accelerator.'

pscustomobject - [pscustomobject] $ hashtable

If we do this and show the results of what we previously had with Get-Member, you will notice a wild difference. The generic methods and properties of a hash table and the specified properties (color, transfer and whether it is convertible or not) are finished.

# OTHER POWERSHELL COMMANDS

S ome people are really excited to see what the difference is between a script and an application. In general, the scripts are small and perform a very precise action. The applications are (relatively) large and bring together innumerable functions.

Consider the approach to providing functions in Microsoft Word as opposed to how similar functions are represented as a set of scripts.

In Word, the number of words is continuously displayed in the status bar at the bottom of the edit window.

You can click on it and get more detailed statistics (one of the many thousands of functions in Microsoft Word).

In PowerShell scripts, you use two separate cmdlets to achieve this functionality:

- Get-Content
- Measure-Object

Get-Content imports a text file as an object (everything in PowerShell is an object), and Measure-Object then collects the statistics on the object for us.

When you put it together, you have:

Get-Content c: \ documents \ myfile.txt |

Measurement-object-word

The character '|' Between the two commands is the 'pipe,' which indicates that instead of viewing the output of the 'Get-Content' command in the PowerShell command window, this data must be passed to the next script cmdlet (Measure-Object).

Now you could look at this example and think, 'This is a very complicated way to find out how many words are in a file.' and you wouldn't be wrong. But the most important thing is that scripting doesn't work.

Instead of importing a single file, we can write a novel with 60 different chapters (one chapter per file). We could put all these files together and pass the result to Measure-Object and get a word count for the whole book at once.

**Use of the pipeline**

As a more practical example of using piping for sysadmin activities, let's try to find and restart a service using PowerShell.

For this we use two cmdlets:

- Get-Service
- Restart-Service

In the beginning, we can follow the steps as if we were doing everything manually. We are looking first for the Windows audio service.

Get the name of the  audiosrv service. If you are in PowerShell (look for the PS prompt), you should get the following:

If we have determined that the service is available, we can restart it.

Restart the name of the audiosrv service.

If we use pipelines, we can instead direct the entire object to the Restart-Service cmdlet.

Get the name of the service audiosrv | Restart-Service

The above is functionally the same but is done as a single command.

To extend it further, we can use the '-PassThru' command to continue guiding the input object through each script.

Get the name of the service audiosrv | Restart service

-PassThru | stop Service

In this way, we can apply a series of commands to the same initial object. Now for a more realistic example:

To begin with, we have a set of computer hostnames (one per line) in a text file.

The first instinct would be to pass the file directly to the Test-Connection cmdlet, e.g. Get-Content -Path C: \ Example.txt | Test-Connection

However, we still need to know what type of object is being passed. The above is passed in the file as if it were a chapter of a book. First, we need to format the file data in the expected format.

To find out, let's take a look at the Get-Help cmdlet.

**Get-Help -Name -Full connection test**

'Complete' indicates that parameter lists should not only contain names and usage but also if and in what format pipeline entries are accepted.

In the screenshot above you see 'Accept pipeline input?' is True and indicates that input via a property name (instead of an object) is accepted.

Each line of the input file is extracted and converted to a property name using the PSCustom Object command (as required by the Test-Connection cmdlet).

Get-Content -Path C: \ Example.txt | ForEach-Object

{[pscustomobject] @ {ComputerName = $ PSItem}} | Test-Connection

## Inputs and outputs of the PowerShell pipeline

For many developers, understanding pipelining in PowerShell is like understanding reductive physicalism. You think you've just gotten it, and therefore the blue screens of the brain. Michael Sorens is inspired by his various efforts to explain the pipelines on StackOverflow to try the simple final explanation for the rest of us.

Pipelining is an important technique when performing the operation you are performing, e.g. For example, reading files of indefinite length or processing collections of large objects must save memory resources by dividing a large activity into its atomic components. If you make a mistake, you won't get this advantage. While PowerShell offers a wide range of pipelining constructs, it's too easy to write code that simply doesn't create a pipeline at all.

## Why Is Pipelining So Important?

As already mentioned, pipelining is useful for saving memory resources. Suppose we want to edit the text in a large file. Without a pipeline effect, you can read the large file in memory, edit the corresponding lines and rewrite the file on your hard drive. If it's big enough, you may not have enough memory to read the whole thing.

Pipelining can significantly improve actual performance.

Instructions in a pipeline are executed simultaneously, even if you have only one processor. For example, if one process crashes while reading most of the file, another process in the pipeline can mean a unit of work.

Pipelining can have a significant impact on end-user experience and significantly improve perceived performance. If the end-user runs a series of commands that last 60 seconds, the user without the pipeline will not see anything until the end of those 60 seconds, while the pipeline output may appear within a few seconds.

To make pipelining as simple as possible, I will present a simple pipeline that routes an input sequence through three consecutive functions and maps an input sequence to an output sequence.

# UNDERSTANDING OF POWERSHELL FOREACH LOOP AND FOREACH-OBJECT

The Microsoft PowerShell scripting language uses cmdlets to do three things: Gather information, set information and delete information. In addition to the cmdlets, PowerShell also offers the ability to process information multiple times. There are two integrated PowerShell features used by most PowerShell administrators. They are 'ForEach-Loop' and 'ForEach-Object.' The PowerShell ForEach cycle allows you to scroll through a series of items collected in a PowerShell variable. For example, you can use the Get-ADUser PowerShell cmdlet to collect information about users from Active Directory. If you need to review each user's city ownership before taking any action, you can use the ForEach Loop. The ForEach object can be used to work directly with objects and is mainly used in a pipeline, as explained in this section. We should investigate a few models where the ForEach Loop and ForEach-Object capacities are used.

**Powershell Foreach Loop**

Our first example of using the ForEach Loop is to verify the city properties of Active Directory users and then take action. Let's say we want to export users whose city ownership is set to London and then save the result to a CSV file. Here is the PowerShell script:

$ CityReport = "C: \ Temp \ CityReport.CSV"

Remove-Item $ CityReport -ErrorAction SilentlyContinue

$ STR = "username, city"

```
Include content $ CityReport $ STR

$ AllUsersNow = Get-ADUser - Filter * - SearchBase

"OU = TestUsers, DC = TechGenix, DC = Com" - Properties *

Foreach ($ ThisUser in $ AllUsersNow)

{

$ CityOfUser = $ ThisUser.City

$ ThisUserNow = $ ThisUser.CN

In the event that ($ CityOfUser - eq "London")

{

$ STRNew = $ ThisUserNow + "," + $ CityOfUser

Include content $ CityReport $ STRNew

}

}
```

As should be obvious in the content above, we have made a variable called $

The City Report which stores the way to the CSV document where the report is saved. We then collect all users from a specific organizational unit and save registered users with all properties in the $ AllUsersNow variable. Next, the processing of the ForEach cycle begins. In the ForEach loop function, we check the user's city property and then use an IF condition to check if the city property contains the 'London' value for the current user or not. If the user registers 'London' as a value in the city property, The current customer name and city name are added to the document C: \ Temp \CityReport.CSV.

Another case of using ForEach Loop is the handling of data put away in a CSV document. Assume we have a CSV document that contains the username, city and division esteems. You need to change the client's city and division properties in the CSV record. To do this, using the accompanying PowerShell content:

$ UserData = "C: \ Temp \ UserData.CSV"

$ CSVFile = Import-CSV $ UserData

Foreach ($ ThisUser in $ CSVFile)

{

$ ModifyThisUser = $ ThisUser

$ NewDepartment = $ ThisUser.Department

$ NewCity = $ ThisUser.City

Set-ADUser -Identity $ ModifyThisUser -City $ Newcity

Set-ADUser -Identity $ ModifyThisUser -Department $

NewDepartment}

**Powershell Foreach Loop**

As should be obvious in the content above, we have imported the substance of the CSV record into the $ CSVFile variable. So, we use the ForEach loop to store the department and city values from the CSV file in the variables $ NewDepartment and $ NewCity, and then we use the Set –ADUser PowerShell cmdlet. We update the department and city values for the user.

In short, use PowerShell ForEach Loop when you need to process information multiple times when you need to act on a certain element based on the property value and/or when you need to edit object information from a file.

In addition to the ForEach Loop function, PowerShell also offers ForEach Object. As the name suggests, the ForEach object works legitimately with objects and is mostly used in a pipeline. For instance, as should be obvious in the accompanying command, the Get-Process cmdlet gets all the data, processes on the local computer and the ForEach object after the pipeline (|) has processed the objects (process names), so it only shows the process name in the output window.

Get-Process | ForEach-Object {$ _. Process name}

To view the process name together with the process ID, run the following command:

Get-Process | ForEach-Object {$ _. ProcessName, $ _. ID}

Another example of using ForEach-Object is to get the length of the considerable number of records in a catalog. Assume we need to check the length of all records in the C: \ Temp folder. You will run these commands:

$ ThisDir = "C: \ Temp" Get-ChildItem $ ThisDir | ForEach-Object – Process {if (!

$ _. PSIsContainer) {$ _. a name; $ _. Length / 1024; ""}}

In the following PowerShell ForEach-Object example, you capture events from the application event log and save the event message to a text file.

## Regular expressions with Windows PowerShell

Windows PowerShell is a Microsoft programming language developed primarily for system administration. Since PowerShell is based on the .NET Framework, PowerShell programmers also offer excellent support for regular expressions in .NET.

## PowerShell operators match and replace

You can use the -match operator to quickly check if a regular expression matches a part of a string. For example, 'test' -match '\ w' returns true because \ w matches t in the test.

As a side effect, the -match operator specifies a special variable called $ match. This is an associative matrix that contains the entire regex match and all the acquisitions group matches. $ Matches [0] gives you the general regex match, $ match [1] the first acquisition group, and $ match ['name'] the text that corresponds to the group named 'name.'

The '–place' operator uses a regular expression to find and replace it with a string. For example, 'test' -replace '\ w', '$ & $ &' returns 'tteesstt'. The regex \ w corresponds to a letter. The replacement text re-inserts the regex match twice with $ &. The replacement text parameter must be specified, and regex and replacement must be separated by a comma. If you don't want to replace regex matches with anything, pass an empty string in place.

By default, regular expressions are case sensitive. This also applies to the .NET Framework. However, this is not the case in PowerShell. -match and -replace are not case sensitive, just like -imatch and -ireplace. Use -cmatch and -creplace to distinguish between uppercase and lowercase letters. I always recommend using the prefix 'i' or 'c' to avoid confusion about the distinction between upper and lower case.

Operators do not provide a way to pass options from the .NET RegexOptions enumeration. Instead, use mode modifiers in the regular expression. For example, (? M) ^ test $ is equivalent to using ^ test $ with RegexOptions.MultiLine passed to the Regex () constructor. Mode modifiers take precedence over externally set options for the regular expression. -cmatch '(?i) test' is not case sensitive, while -imatch '(? -i) test' is case sensitive.

The mode modifier replaces the preference for the -match operator.

**Replace the Text as a Literal String**

The -replace operator supports the same placeholders for replacement texts for the Regex.Replace () function in .NET. $ & is the general regex match, $ 1 is the text corresponding to the first acquisition group, and $ {name} is the text corresponding to the group named 'name.'

However, PowerShell has one further limitation: Strings in speech marks use dollar syntax for variable interpolation. Variable interpolation takes place before the Regex. Replace () function (which –replace uses internally) parses the replacement text. Unlike Perl, $ 1 in PowerShell is not a magical variable. This syntax only works in the replacement text. The-place operator doesn't set the $ match variable either. The effect is that 'test' -replace '(\ w) (\ w),' "$ 2 $ 1" (speech marks) returns the empty string (provided that you have the variables $ 1 and $ 2 in the previous PowerShell Code not specified). Due to variable interpolation, the Replace () function never sees $ 2 $ 1. Use 'test' -replace '(\ w) (\ w)', '$ 2 $ 1' (replace with quotation marks) or 'test' -replace '(\ w) so that the Replace () function can replace its placeholders. (\ w) ', "' $ 2 '$ 1" (backtick escaped dollars) to ensure that $ 2 $ 1 is literally passed to Regex.Replace ().

**Use the System.Text.RegularExpressions.Regex class**

To take advantage of all the .NET regex processing features with PowerShell, create a regular expression object by instantiating the System.Text.RegularExpressions.Regex class. PowerShell provides a handy link if you want to use the Regex () constructor, which uses a regular expression string as its only parameter. $ regex = [regex] '\ W +' compiles the regular expression \ W + (which corresponds to one or more non-word characters) and stores the result in the $ regex variable. Now you can call all the methods of the Regex class for your $ regex object.

Splitting a string is a common activity for which PowerShell does not have an integrated operator. With the regex object we just created, we can $ regex. Call Split ('This is a test') to get an array of all the words in the string.

If you want to use a different constructor, you must use the PowerShell New Object cmdlet. For example, to set the

RegexOptions.MultiLine flag, the following line of code is needed:

$ regex = new System.Text.RegularExpressions.Regex object ('^ test $',

[System.Text.RegularExpressions.RegexOptions]:: multiline).

However, the use of mode modifiers within the regular expression is a much shorter and more readable solution:

$ regex = [regex] '(? m) ^ test $'

# WINDOWS POWERSHELL PROVIDERS

Access to data storage in Windows PowerShell depends on the provider. As mentioned earlier, the provider is a .NET program that allows you to access data in a data store and then view or modify it.

Use the Get-PSProvider cmdlet to find the providers available on a computer. To find all available providers, simply enter the following:

Get-PSProvider

To view an alphabetical list of PowerShell providers, type: Get-psprovider | Name of the sort object the storage of party data.

Alias of Windows PowerShell

Certificate X509 certified for digital signatures

Environment Windows environment variables

File system File system drives, folders (directories) and files

Function Windows PowerShell functions

Windows registry

Windows PowerShell variable

In general, each provider supports the display of its data, just like a traditional Windows command shell displays the file system data. However, there are differences in the details. For example, the alias provider does not support hierarchical data because there is no concept for an aliased folder.

Integrated Windows PowerShell providers are included in snap-ins (which may also include cmdlets).

**Windows PowerShell remote controls**

The Windows PowerShell remote service provides a method for passing a local execution command to a remote computer. The commands must not be available on the computer you are connecting to. It is sufficient that only remote computers can execute commands.

The Windows PowerShell remote service is based on the WS-Man (Web Services Management) protocol. WS-Management is an open Distributed Management Task Force (DMTF) standard that depends on the HTTP (or HTTPS) protocol. The Windows Remote Management (WinRM) administration is the Microsoft usage of WS-Management. WinRM is at the heart of the Windows PowerShell remote service. However, this service can also be used by other non-PowerShell applications. The remote service is enabled by default on Windows Server 2012 and must communicate with other Windows servers from the Server Manager console and even connect to the local computer on which the console is running. Remoting is not enabled by default on client operating systems such as Windows 7 or Windows 8.

After activation, the remote-control registers at least one listener. Each listener accepts incoming traffic over HTTP or HTTPS.

Listeners can be associated with one or more IP addresses. Incoming traffic indicates the intended destination or endpoint. These endpoints are otherwise called session configurations.

At the point when traffic is coordinated to an endpoint, WinRM begins the PowerShell engine, discharges approaching traffic, releases incoming traffic, and waits for PowerShell to complete its task. PowerShell then passes the results to WinRM, and WinRM transfers this data to the computer from which the commands come.

**Establishing an Interactive PowerShell Console on a Remote System**

An interactive PowerShell console can be accessed on a remote system using the 'Enter-PsSession' command. It looks a bit like SSH. Similar to Invoke-Command, Enter-PsSession can be run as a current user or using alternative credentials from a non-domain system.

**Exit-PSSession**

Create background sessions

There is another interesting feature of PowerShell

Remoting that allows users to create sessions in the background using the New-PsSession command. Background sessions can be useful when you want to run multiple commands on many systems. Like other commands, the New-PsSession command can be run as a current user or using alternative credentials from a non-domain system. Examples below.

New-PSSession -ComputerName server1.domain.com

server1.domain.com –Credentials domain \ serveradmin

New-PSSession –ComputerName

When the ActiveDirectory PowerShell module is installed, you can create background sessions for many systems simultaneously (but it can be done in many ways). Below is an example of a command showing how to create background sessions for all domain systems. The example tells the best way to do this from a non-space framework with elective area qualifications.

New-PSDrive -PSProvider ActiveDirectory -Name RemoteADS

-Root "" server a.b.c.d -credential domain \ user

cd RemoteADS:

Get-ADComputer -Filter * -Properties name | Choose @

{Name = "Computer name"; Expression = {$ _. "Name"}} |

New-PSSession

List background sessions

Once some sessions are set up, they can be viewed using the Get-PsSession command.

Get-PSSession

Interact with background sessions

When I first used this feature, it felt like I was working with metasploit sessions, but these sessions are somewhat more stable.

Below is an example of how to interact with an active session using the session

ID.

Enter-PsSession –id 3

Use the Exit-PsSession command to end the session. This will put the session back in the background.

Exit-PSSession

Run commands through background sessions

If you want to run a command for all active sessions, the

"Invoke-Command" and "Get-PsSession" commands can be used together. Below is an example.

Invoke-Command -Session (Get-PSSession) –ScriptBlock {hostname}

Remove background sessions

To remove all active sessions, you can use the

"Disconnect-PsSession" command, as shown below.

Get-PSSession | Disconnect-PSSession

**Windows PowerShell Workflows**

A workflow is a series of scheduled and connected steps that perform long-lasting tasks or require coordination of multiple steps on multiple managed devices or nodes.

The advantages of a workflow compared to a normal script include the ability to perform an action for multiple devices simultaneously and the ability to automatically correct errors. A Windows PowerShell workflow is a Windows PowerShell script used by the Windows Workflow Foundation. While the workflow is written using Windows PowerShell syntax and started from Windows PowerShell, it is processed by the Windows Workflow Foundation.

**Basic Structure**

A Windows PowerShell workflow begins with the Workflow keyword, followed by the script text in curly braces. The workflow name follows the keyword's workflow, as shown in the following syntax. The workflow name corresponds to the name of the automation runbook.

Workflow test runbook

```
{

<Command>

}
```

To add parameters to the work process, use the Param keyword (see the syntax below). The administration portal asks the user to enter values for these parameters when starting the runbook. This example uses the optional parameter attribute that indicates whether the parameter is mandatory or not.

**Workflow test runbook**

```
{

param

(

[Parameters (mandatory = <$ True | $ False>]

[Type] $ <parameter name>,

[Parameters (mandatory = <$ True | $ False>]

[Type] $ <parameter name>

)

<Command>

}
```

**Designation**

The workflow name must match the verbal-noun format, which is standard in Windows PowerShell. For a rundown of endorsed action words to use, see approved action words for Windows PowerShell directions. The name of the work process must match the name of the robotization runbook. When the runbook is imported, the file name must match the workflow name and end with .ps1.

**Activities**

An activity is a specific action in a workflow. Just as a script is made up of one or more commands, a workflow is made up of one or more tasks performed in a sequence. The Windows PowerShell workflow automatically converts many of the Windows PowerShell cmdlets into activities when a workflow is running. If you specify one of these cmdlets in the runbook, the corresponding task is actually performed by the Windows Workflow Foundation.

For detailed information on general workflow parameters, see about_WorkflowCommonParameters.

**Integration Module**

An incorporation module is a bundle that contains a Windows PowerShell module and can be brought into computerization. Items and administrations, for example, Operations Manager and Azure have modules that contain explicit cmdlets for their activities.

The incorporation modules that are brought into the computerization are naturally accessible for all Runbooks. Since robotization depends on Windows PowerShell 4.0, it underpins programmed stacking of modules so that cmdlets from introduced modules can be used without bringing them into the content using the import modules.

Any Windows PowerShell module can be brought into robotization as long as all conditions are in a solitary organizer. On the off chance that the module relies upon library settings or records that are not in the default area, it very well may be imported, yet doubtlessly it won't work since computerization can't discover the conditions. Modules with outside conditions can be utilized in a runbook by introducing them to another host and afterward getting to them with an InlineScript content square.

With Service Management Automation, modules with outer conditions can be utilized by introducing them on each activity server. The cmdlets in these modules can be used in runbooks, yet are not perceived via robotization to help capacities, for example, the undertaking addition wizard.

To use this function, you can use the 'New SmaPortableModule' cmdlet to create a portable module. This cmdlet creates a module that contains a stub for each of its cmdlets, and that can be imported into automation. If a runbook uses one of these cmdlets, the stub forwards the call to the actual cmdlet in the external module. This module must be installed on each working server; otherwise, the call will fail.

**Parallel Execution**

An advantage of Windows PowerShell workflows is the ability to run a series of commands in parallel, rather than sequentially, as with a typical script. This is particularly useful in runbooks because they may require several actions that take a long time to complete. For example, a runbook can provide a number of virtual machines. Instead of running each deployment process sequentially, actions could be performed simultaneously to increase overall efficiency. The runbook continues only when all are complete.

The parallel keyword allows you to create a script block with multiple commands executed simultaneously. This uses the syntax shown below. In this case, activity1 and activity2 are started simultaneously.

Activity 3 starts only after completing activity one and activity 2.

parallel

{

<Activity1>

<Activity2>

}

<Activity3>

With the ForEach - Parallel construct, you can process commands for each element in a collection simultaneously. The objects in the assortment are prepared in equal, while the commands in the content square are executed consistently. This uses the syntax shown below. In this case, Activity1 starts simultaneously for all items in the collection. For each element, Activity2 starts when Activity1 ends. Activity 3 starts only after completing activity one and activity 2 for all items.

For each parallel ($ <item> in $ <collection>)

{

<Activity1>

<Activity2>

}

<Activity3>

The Sequence keyword is used to execute commands one after the other in a parallel script block. The sequence script block is executed in parallel with other instructions, but the instructions within the block are executed in sequence. This uses the syntax shown below. In this case, activity1, activity2, and activity3 are started simultaneously. Activity 4 starts only after activity three has completed. Activity 5 will begin after all other activities have been completed.

parallel

{

<Activity1>

<Activity2>

sequence

{

<Activity3>

<Activity4>

}

}

<Activity5>

Checkpoints

A checkpoint is a preview of the present condition of the work process that contains the present an incentive for the factors and all the output generated up to that point. The last checkpoint to be run in a runbook is saved in the automation database so that the workflow can continue even if an error occurs. Checkpoint data is removed at the end of the runbook process.

You can use the Checkpoint workflow activity to define a checkpoint in a workflow. If you include this activity in a runbook, a checkpoint is immediately created. If the runbook is interrupted by an error and the job continues, it will resume from the point of the last specified checkpoint.

In the accompanying example code, a mistake happens after Activity2, which causes the runbook to stop. If the job continues, Activity2 will run first because it was immediately after the last specified checkpoint.

<Activity1>

Checkpoint workflow

<Activity2>

<Error>

<Activity3>

Checkpoints must be set in a runbook for activities that may be subject to errors and should not be repeated if the runbook continues.

For example, the runbook can create a virtual machine. You can set a checkpoint both before and after the virtual machine creation commands. If compilation fails, the commands are repeated when the runbook continues. If the compilation is successful, but the runbook fails later, the virtual machine will not be rebuilt if the runbook continues.

**Attach A Runbook**

You can force a runbook to expose itself to the Pause Workflow activity. This activity sets a checkpoint and causes the workflow to stop immediately. Suspending a workflow is useful for runbooks, which may require you to manually perform a step before performing other tasks.

**InlineScript**

The InlineScript activity executes a command block in a separate session with no workflow and returns the output to the workflow. While the commands in a workflow are sent to the Windows Workflow Foundation for processing, the commands are processed in an InlineScript block by Windows PowerShell. The activity uses general standard workflow parameters, including PSComputerName and PSCredential, which you can use to specify that the code block should be run on another computer or use alternative credentials.

InlineScript uses the syntax shown below.

Inline

{

<Script block>

} <General parameters>

InlineScript is most commonly used in a runbook to execute a block of code on another computer. This is necessary if the cmdlets in the runbook are not installed in automation or if the action has only permissions that can be performed locally on the target computer. This is shown in the following figure.

## Inline Chart Script

To perform the code lock on another computer, the PSComputer and PSCredential parameters are used for the InlineScript activity.

A worldwide resource, for example, a certification or a connection, is typically used in a runbook to provide values for these parameters. The following sample code executes a series of commands on a computer represented by a connection called 'MyConnection.'

$ con = Get-AutomationConnection -Name 'MyConnection'

$ Securepassword = ConvertTo-SecureString -AsPlainText

-String $ con.Password -Force

$ cred = New-Object -TypeName

System.Management.Automation.PSCredential          -ArgumentList $ con.Username, $

Securepassword

Inline

{

\<Command>

} "PSComputer $ con.ComputerName" PSCredential

$ cred

Although InlineScript activities may be critical in some runbooks, they should only be used when needed for the following reasons:

- Checkpoints cannot be used within an InlineScript block.
- If an error occurs within the block, you must continue from the beginning.
- InlineScript affects the scalability of the runbook because it contains the Windows PowerShell session for the entire length of the InlineScript block.
- Activities such as Get-AutomationVariable
- Get-AutomationPSCredential are not available in an InlineScript block.

This offers the accompanying favorable circumstances:

You can see the working process after each stress. If the activity is interrupted or delayed and continues, the cycle can continue.

You can use 'Parallel' ForEach for processing collectibles at the same time.

Consider the following tips when using InlineScript in the runbook:

However, you can pass values to the script using the $ Using scope modifier. For example, a variable called $ abc that was set outside of InlineScript would become $ using: abc in an InlineScript.

To return the output from an InlineScript, assign the output to a variable and send all the data to be returned to the output stream.

In the following example, the string "hi" is assigned the string

"hi".

$ output = InlineScript {Writing-Output "hi"}

Avoid defining job streams in the InlineScript area.

Although some workflows may work properly, this is not a tested scenario. As a result, confusing error messages or unexpected behavior can occur.